Math Around Us

Using Addition at Home

Tracey Steffora

Heinemann Library
Chicago, Illinois

www.capstonepub.com
Visit our website to find out more information about Heinemann-Raintree books.

To order:

☎ Phone 800-747-4992

💻 Visit www.capstonepub.com to browse our catalog and order online.

© 2011 Heinemann Library
an imprint of Capstone Global Library, LLC
Chicago, Illinois

Edited by Rebecca Rissman, Tracey Steffora, and Catherine Veitch
Designed by Joanna Hinton-Malivoire
Picture research by Elizabeth Alexander
Production by Victoria Fitzgerald
Originated by Capstone Global Library Ltd

Library of Congress Cataloging-in-Publication Data
Steffora, Tracey.
  Using addition at home / Tracey Steffora.
     p. cm.—(Math around us)
  Includes bibliographical references and index.
  ISBN 978-1-4329-4924-2 (hc)—ISBN 978-1-4329-4932-7
(pb) 1. Addition—Juvenile literature. I. Title.
  QA115.S7775 2011
  513.2′11—dc22   2010030761

Acknowledgments
The author and publisher are grateful to the following for permission to reproduce photographs: Alamy: Barry Lewis, 5 bottom left, Design Pics, 19, 23 top, ImagesBazaar, 14, Jon Arnold Images Ltd, 5 top right, Loop Images Ltd, 4 bottom left, Photo Network, 4 top left, Randy Romano, 4 bottom right; Getty Images Inc.: Bloomimage, 10, Jam Photography, 15, 23 bottom, Jon Feingersh Photography Inc, 11; Shutterstock: ESB Professional, cover, 5 top left, 18, Juice Flair, back cover, 7, Monkey Business Images, 6, Pressmaster, 5 bottom right, Vasina Natalia, 22

We would like to thank Nancy Harris, Dee Reid, and Diana Bentley for their assistance in the preparation of this book.

Contents

Around the World

People live in homes.

At home we share meals with family and friends.

One More

Four people are sharing a meal.

There is a knock on the door.

It is a friend!

start with

add

How many people are there in all?

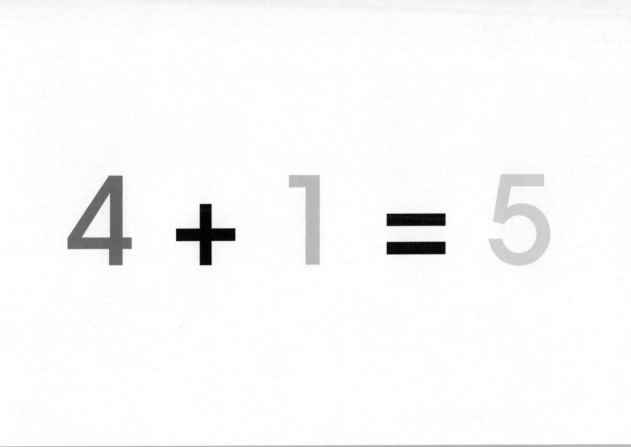

Four plus one equals five.

There are five people in all.

Two More

Four people are sharing a meal.

The phone rings.

Grandma and Grandpa are coming over!

start with

add

How many people are there in all?

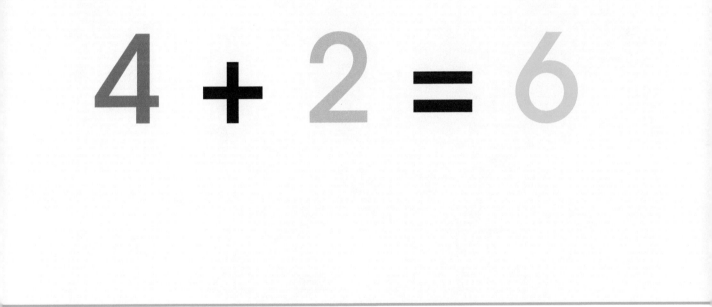

4 + 2 = 6

Four plus two equals six.

There are six people in all.

Three More

Four people are sharing a meal.

They get a text.

Three friends are coming over!

start with

add

How many people are there in all?

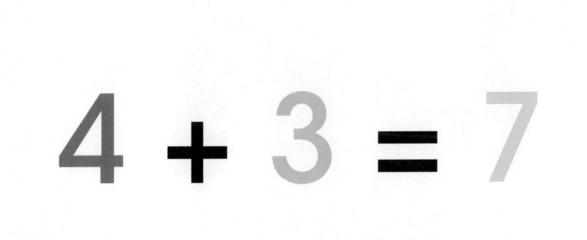

$$4 + 3 = 7$$

Four plus three equals seven.

There are seven people in all.

Four More

Four people are making a meal.

They get an email.

Four more people are coming over!

start with

add

How many people are there in all?

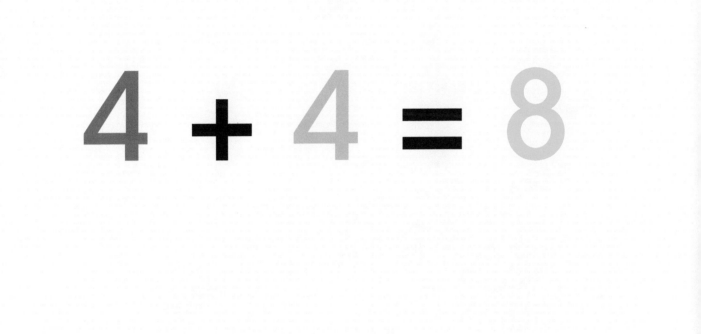

4 + 4 = 8

Four plus four equals eight.

There are eight people in all.

Clean Up

Sharing a meal is fun. But the dishes also add up!

Picture Glossary

email a message sent or received through a computer; electronic mail

text a message sent or received through a cellular phone

Index

Notes to Parents and Teachers
Before reading
Discuss with children different activities that occur at home. They might mention having meals, playing with toys, doing laundry, etc. Encourage them to describe what happens during each activity and then review and highlight any language or description that implies addition (e.g., add laundry soap to the wash, put forks and spoons on the table). Remind them that they use addition every day, even when they are not aware of it.

After reading
To help give children a concrete sense of addition, you might have them act out some of the addition stories in this text. For example, four children could be sitting at a table, and then another child knocks on the door. Review how they can tell this story using numbers and symbols (4+1=5). Encourage them to create their own scenarios with different quantities of children and record their stories with words, drawings and/or equations.